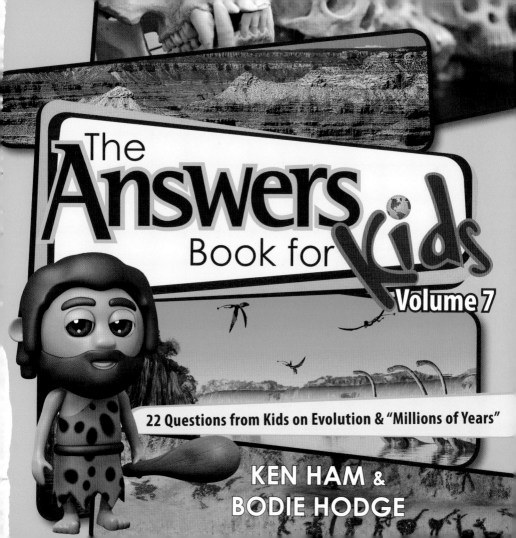

The Answers Book for Kids

Volume 7

22 Questions from Kids on Evolution & "Millions of Years"

KEN HAM & BODIE HODGE

First Printing: November 2017

Master Books®
P.O. Box 726
Green Forest, AR 72638

Master Books® is a division of the New Leaf Publishing Group, Inc.

Printed in China

Book design by Terry White

ISBN 13: 978-1-68344-066-6
ISBN 13: 978-1-61458-630-2 (digital)
Library of Congress Control Number: 2017952422

All Scripture references are New King James Version unless otherwise noted.

Please visit our website for other great titles: www.masterbooks.com

When you see this icon, there will be related Scripture references noted for parents to use in answering their children's, and even their own, questions.

For Parents and Teachers

Therefore whoever hears these sayings of Mine, and does them, I will liken him to a wise man who built his house on the rock: and the rain descended, the floods came, and the winds blew and beat on that house; and it did not fall, for it was founded on the rock (Matthew 7:24-25).

Dear parents:

As we dive into this final book of the series, let's reflect on the previous books' questions. There were multitudes of them! Kids have a lot of questions and this is a good thing. So we really need to be diligent in giving them biblical answers.

Regardless of the questions children may ask, we want to encourage you to open the Bible and search for the correct answer. This is what we love to do. And our hope is that you will have that same love for truth of the Bible. God's Word is always true and this is something in which we can rest assured.

When it comes to Satan and angels, God is our only reliable source of information. Are you ready to see the questions we received from the kids? Here we go!

Blessings in Christ,

Ken and Bodie

Question: How old is the earth and universe?

Kylie

Age 6

4

Answer:

In the beginning God created the heavens and the earth (Genesis 1:1).

God, who knows all things, knows how old the earth and universe are. Brilliantly, He gave us a "birth certificate" when He created them. They were created on the first day of creation.

If we add up the next 5 days, we get to the creation of Adam. He was the first man. So far, that is only 6 days. Then when we add up how old people were, like Adam and his son Seth, we can get a timeline. Adam was 130 years old when he had Seth. Then you add 105 years because that is how old Seth was when he had his son Enosh. If you keep doing this, you get about 2,000 years from Adam to Abraham.

Everyone agrees that Abraham lived about 2,000 years before Jesus, and Jesus lived about 2,000 years ago. So if you add up 6 days + 2,000 years (from Adam to Abraham) + 2,000 years (from Abraham to Christ) + 2,000 years (from Jesus until today), you get about 6,000 years. So when you start with the Bible, the earth and universe are only about 6,000 years old.

John 1:1; Exodus 20:11

Question:

Why do teachers and textbooks keep saying "millions of years ago"?

Madeline G.

Answer:

Train up a child in the way he should go, and when he is old he will not depart from it (Proverbs 22:6).

In most cases, the teachers are required to say such things. This is because the state religion is secular humanism (think atheism, where man says "God does not exist"). This religion recently began to dominate the USA, England, and many other places, like France, Germany, and Australia.

When the government gives money to education or museums, they require their religion to be presented. This is why we see evolution and millions of years in state-sponsored museums like the natural history museums, state schools, and other government-funded projects.

This is why textbooks in state schools speak of millions of years and evolution. There are textbooks that do not have those things in them, but you don't find them in state-run schools. Evolution, millions of years, and the big bang are part of the religion of humanism/atheism. In the same way, six-day creation, the Fall of mankind into sin, and the Flood of Noah are a part of Christianity.

It is a battle over two different religions. Sadly, teachers are stuck in the middle of this debate.

Deuteronomy 11:19; Proverbs 9:9;
Matthew 28:19–20

Question:

Who started the idea of evolution?

Gershom & Paige

Age 8 & 9

8

Answer:

You alone are the LORD; You have made heaven, the heaven of heavens, with all their host, the earth and everything on it, the seas and all that is in them, and You preserve them all. The host of heaven worships You (Exodus 33:20).

Some of the first evolutionists were Greeks called the Epicureans. They lived after the Old Testament was already written! They believed things evolved from tiny particles. Paul proved them wrong in Acts 17, and this view basically died for 1,800 years.

Around 1800, a man named Jean Lamarck brought back a type of evolution called Lamarckian evolution. Then later in 1859, Charles Darwin came up with a different type of evolution based on *natural selection*. But that still didn't make evolution happen. Even some in the church began to believe in evolution.

Most evolutionists now believe in "neo-Darwinism" or "new-evolution." They say *natural selection + mutations* will lead to evolution (new and better animals and plants). But that still doesn't work when we watch things in nature. Mutations cause big problems in creatures, like defects, cancer, and missing body parts! So things are NOT getting better with mutations.

So even though a lot of people believe evolution, it still doesn't work. It is better to trust in God's Word and realize that God specially created things. This would be an easy job for an all-powerful God.

Colossians 1:16; Hebrews 1:1–2

Question: Why do people think the earth (and everything else) came from nothing?

Eve

Age 8

10

Answer:

"For since the creation of the world His invisible attributes are clearly seen, being understood by the things that are made, even His eternal power and Godhead, so that they are without excuse (Romans 1:20).

Sadly, there are people who do not like God and the Bible, so they try to invent a different history than what God teaches in His Word. They make up a story to try to satisfy their understanding of the past.

By doing this, the people are ignoring what really happened at creation. This is called "suppressing the truth." God says that when they do this, they have no excuse.

Since some people do not want all things to come from God, then from where do things come? Believe it or not, they have little choice but to say that "all things come from nothing" — all by themselves!

It sounds crazy, doesn't it? We don't see things coming from nothing. But this is what some people have to believe in order to reject God. This "suppression of the truth" should be a reminder to us that we should always trust God's Word in all subjects — especially creation — as the Lord will never be wrong.

Romans 1:18–19; Psalm 14:1

Question: Why is belief in evolution more popular than creation?

Levi

Age 9

12

Answer:

Enter by the narrow gate; for wide is the gate and broad is the way that leads to destruction, and there are many who go in by it (Matthew 7:13).

Evolution is not necessarily more popular than creation. In fact, more Americans believe creation than evolution. But in some places, it is true that evolution is more popular. One of those places is England, where Charles Darwin, the founder of modern evolution, lived. Broad (large) is the path to destruction in England right now!

Sadly, the governments of many places like England and the United States impose the religion of evolution on many kids. We see this in state schools and state-funded museums.

We also see this influence of evolution by media (news people for example) who believe in evolution. We even see it in many movies — especially kid movies! Even many Disney® movies, which are geared toward families, have evolution in them.

As Christians, we need to recognize that this religion of evolution is a *false* religion and God's Word is true. We need to be on lookout for this religion so we can spot it and not be deceived by it.

2 Timothy 3:13; James 1:16

13

Question: How did people get the idea that we evolved from fish, frogs, and "apemen"?

Nancy K.

Age 8

14

Answer:

Professing to be wise, they became fools, and changed the glory of the incorruptible God into an image made like corruptible man — and birds and four-footed animals and creeping things (Romans 1:22–23).

There are two reasons evolutionists believe we evolved from "lower life forms." First, evolutionists think that all things evolved from a simple, singled-celled organism (or something like it) — similar to an amoeba. By the way, these single-celled organisms are not simple, but complex little biological factories!

Evolutionists believe that this amoeba-like creature had to evolve into higher organisms until man. But we don't observe this, so it is not science, but a story like a fairy tale.

The second reason is due to the rock layers that have fossils. Evolutionists believe the rocks were formed slowly over millions of years. They believe each layer was a time period a long time ago. The rock layers have sea creatures, then amphibians, then reptiles, and lastly mammals (there are many exceptions to this, by the way). So they assume that man had to evolve through what was buried in each layer.

However, most of those rock layers were laid down during the Flood of Noah, and it is an order of burial. Sea creatures were first since they live in the ocean; then amphibians and reptiles, which sink when they die; and finally, mammals, which tend to float.

Luke 17:27; Titus 1:14

15

Question: Where did the idea of millions of years come from?

Kylie

Age 6

16

Answer:

And the waters prevailed exceedingly on the earth, and all the high hills under the whole heaven were covered (Genesis 7:19).

As we talked about earlier, a few Greeks believed in an infinite (never ending) past, and the Apostle Paul argues against them in Acts 17. Nobody really believes that anymore. But very few believed in millions of years until about 200 years ago.

People who did not respect God and the Bible said that we should leave out the Bible when we discuss how old the earth is. Scientists started guessing how old the earth was by looking at rock layers. They ignored the Bible's account of the Flood, and assumed the rock layers were laid down slowly over millions of years.

A man named Charles Lyell said the rock layers were evidence of slow build-up of dirt and rock over "millions of years." Lyell said there was no global Flood. Of course, God disagrees with Lyell because God said a Flood covered everything under the heavens. The Flood makes more sense of the rock layers.

But many people were tricked into thinking Lyell was right and that God was wrong. Today, we still have to deal with people falsely believing in millions of years instead of a global Flood.

Genesis 7:20–23

LIES

uninstalling . . .

Question: Why did people start believing in evolution?

Sergio K.

Age 10

Answer:

For if you believed Moses, you would believe Me; for he wrote about Me. But if you do not believe his writings, how will you believe My words? (John 5:46–47).

It is the same reason people start to follow after other false religions — they don't want to follow God and His Word. Sadly, there are many people who don't want to be accountable to God and the Bible. Therefore, they want to give reasons for their unbelief. So they try to reject and ignore the knowledge of God. This means they are willing to believe anything else — including evolution — instead of Genesis.

When evolution began gaining popularity in the 1800s, it gave people an alternative to believing in creation. Many early evolutionists felt like they had a good reason for rejecting God. What they didn't realize was that they are just buying into a false story about the past instead of the truth.

Evolutionists were rejecting Genesis (written by Moses), which explains the foundation of sin. It was Adam's sin that brought death and suffering into the world. Jesus Christ, the Son of God, stepped into history to become a man and die on the Cross. It was Christ taking our punishment that made salvation possible.

Without the creation-gospel message, life is meaningless and hopeless. That is the "fruit" of an evolutionary worldview.

Psalm 119:118; John 14:6

Question: If evolutionists say that dinosaurs evolved into birds, how do they explain birds being here, especially if all the dinosaurs became extinct at the same time from a meteorite that hit earth?

Joy B.

Age Unknown

Answer:

Do not be deceived, my beloved brethren (James 1:16).

The problem here is that different evolutionists believe different things and they don't agree with each other. Some believe the story that dinosaurs turned into birds.

Other evolutionists believe the story about a meteorite (comet/"impactor") that struck the earth and killed the dinosaurs. But these are two different models. Do not be deceived — both of these views are wrong, because God told the true account of history in Genesis 1.

There is evidence of a Theropod dinosaur that ate three birds,[1] so birds and dinosaurs (land animals) were living at the same time — as we expect from six-day creation (Genesis 1:21–25).

The reason dinosaurs have died out is due to sin. With sin in Genesis 3, things began to die and some animals, not just dinosaurs, have gone extinct.

The dinosaur bones we find in the fossil layers are primarily from Noah's Flood. Dinosaurs have died out since the time of the Flood, just like many other animals like dodo birds, saber-toothed cats, and mammoths.

Genesis 7:22; Exodus 23:1

HOLY
BIBLE

Question: Did "cave men" exist?

Annie

Age 10

Answer:

And there he went into a cave, and spent the night in that place; and behold, the word of the LORD came to him, and He said to him, "What are you doing here, Elijah?" (1 Kings 19:9).

I presume this is meant to refer to "missing links" between man and ape-like creatures. In that case, no. Missing links are not going to be found. There are no step-by-step ape-to-human intermediates.

People keep trying to make them though. There are three ways they do this. They take an ape and try to make it look human when they draw it or make a model of it for a museum. This is the case of a famous one called Lucy. Lucy was just an ape, but evolutionists try to make it look human.

The second way is to take a human and make it look like an ape. This is what evolutionists have done with Neanderthals. Neanderthals are human, but they make them look like an intermediate between apes and humans in images and museum models.

The last way evolutionists try to make a missing link is to fake it. This happened with Piltdown man. But people are getting better at fakes, so beware! God made humans and apes distinct on day 6 of creation.

Genesis 1:24–28

23

Question:

Were the continents ever connected?

Annie

Age 10

24

Answer:

Then God said, "Let the waters under the heavens be gathered together into one place, and let the dry land appear"; and it was so (Genesis 1:9).

Most creationists believe there was just one continent in the beginning. They get this from Genesis 1:9. All the water was in one place, so we assume the land was too. Naturally, we cannot be absolutely sure of this, but it seems like a good idea.

Today, we have seven continents. So how did that happen? The evolutionists believe that it happened slowly, with millions of years of slow, gradual movements. Keep in mind this is not science, because science is observable and repeatable.

Creationists believe that the Flood of Noah's day (Genesis 6–8) is what caused the breakup and splitting into the continents of today. The mountains of Ararat (that Noah's Ark landed in) were pushed up as a result of continental collision. Much of the continental movement was done by that stage of the Flood.

It comes down to trusting what God says happened in the past versus the stories that people who oppose God make up about the past. God is never wrong, but imperfect people are wrong about the past far too often.

Genesis 7:11, 8:2

25

THEORY

REALITY

Question: Why do evolutionists keep believing when there is proof it isn't true?

Becca

Age 9

26

Answer:

Take heed to yourselves, lest your heart be deceived, and you turn aside and serve other gods and worship them (Deuteronomy 11:16).

We do not observe the biological changes necessary for evolution. We do not have the billions of missing links that are supposed to be there. It doesn't take millions of years to make oil, coal, petrified wood, rock layers, fossils, canyons, and so on. Without millions of years, there can be no evolution.

People often believe things that they know are not true. Romans 1 shows that people are without excuse, knowing in their hearts (heart often means mind in the Bible) that God created the world. God points out that people "try to hide" this knowledge.

They deceived themselves into believing evolution, and they worship evolution as the truth. The Bible speaks of this unrighteous deception:

And for this reason God will send them strong delusion, that they should believe the lie, that they all may be condemned who did not believe the truth but had pleasure in unrighteousness (2 Thessalonians 2:11–12).

The unrighteous want to be deceived; God permitted them to be deluded by a lie. Unless they repent, they will be judged.

Romans 1:18–21

Question:

Are there different universes?

Annie

Age 10

28

Answer:

In the beginning God created the heavens and the earth (Genesis 1:1).

A multiverse is an idea that there are multiple universes all coexisting at the same time. You need to understand that this is just a strange suggestion (hypothesis) that has no basis in reality.

Based on the Bible, there are good reasons that a multiverse is false anyway. For example, one reason that a few people believe in a multiverse is to downplay our own universe to say ours is not special. However, God created the universe (with phrases like "heavens and earth"). It was specially created, and the earth was specifically designed for life.

For those holding to a multiverse, they presume there was no God and that everything came from nothing, has no purpose, and nothing is special — not even the earth or our universe. So to pretend our universe is not special, they make up a story to say there are a whole lot of universes and ours is just one of many!

God specially created the universe, earth, and man. And Jesus, the Son of God, became a man to save us right here *on this earth in this universe.* That is indeed special!

Isaiah 45:18; 2 Peter 3:10–13

Question: Why did they name the ape "Lucy"?

Eve

Age 8

30

Answer:

So God created man in His own image; in the image of God He created him; male and female He created them (Genesis 1:27).

Lucy was an ape whose fossils were found in Ethiopia in eastern Africa. Lucy's fossil is officially named AL 288-1.

When researchers found the fossils in 1974, there was a song called "Lucy in the Sky with Diamonds," from a famous band called the Beatles. This song was played over and over again in their camp. So they nicknamed the fossils . . . Lucy.

Lucy was found in rock layers that came after the Flood (post-Flood sediment). So Lucy lived after Noah and the Flood. In other words Adam, Eve, and Noah all lived before Lucy, so clearly Lucy isn't a missing link between apes and humans!

Many evolutionists take Lucy and draw it to look "half-human" and "half-ape" because they really want this to be a missing link. We even see artists do this with Lucy in museums too.

However, with an honest look at the fossils, Lucy is just an ape. Its bone measurements are very similar to a chimpanzee. So it is really just a type of chimp that existed post-Flood. This is what we expect — humans are humans and apes are apes.

Genesis 6:20; 1 Corinthians 15:39

Question: Why doesn't God make the evolutionists extinct?

Emma

Age 8

32

Answer:

The Lord is not slack concerning His promise, as some count slackness, but is longsuffering toward us, not willing that any should perish but that all should come to repentance (2 Peter 3:9)."

Be kind! Did you know that all of us fall short of the glory of God (Romans 3:23)? In fact, evolution is just one of many false ideas, but the Lord is patient with us.

God wants evolutionists (and anyone in false religions) to repent and come to know the truth in the Bible. *Repent* means to turn from, and be sorry for sin and false beliefs. God is patient (longsuffering) about this too.

There have been many false religions throughout history, many of which no longer exist. Some false views last longer than others. God's religion, Christianity, will last and the others will eventually fade. The Bible says the Church will prevail (Matthew 16:18). Ultimately, all false worldviews will finally "go extinct" when God creates a new heavens and new earth.

Sometimes we don't understand why God is so patient, but it is comforting to know that God knows what He is doing.

Matthew 16:18; Revelation 21:1, 27

Question: Are some people more evolved than others like different skin tones?

Audrey

Age 10

34

Answer:

And He [God] has made from one blood every nation of men to dwell on all the face of the earth, and has determined their preappointed times and the boundaries of their dwellings (Acts 17:26).

This is a common evolutionary teaching that began with people like Charles Darwin and Ernst Haeckel (a German evolutionist in the 1800s). They taught that as people evolved from apes, some people were more evolved and others were less evolved. Darwin was sure that the "more evolved" race would kill all the other races, as he noted in his book *The Descent of Man.*

The Bible shows that all people are descendants of Adam and Eve, who were our first parents created by God. There is only one race — the human race — or as some people say "Adam's race."

In the New Testament Paul agreed that we are all related when he said all people were from "one blood." We do have variation in our skin tone, but we are basically all a shade of brown (based primarily on our brownish skin pigment called *melanin*), so we are not really red, yellow, black, and white!

Because we are all related, we are all sinners and in need of Jesus Christ no matter what we look like.

Genesis 3:20; 1 Corinthians 15:45

Question: Did God stop creating, or is He still creating today?

J.R.

Age unknown

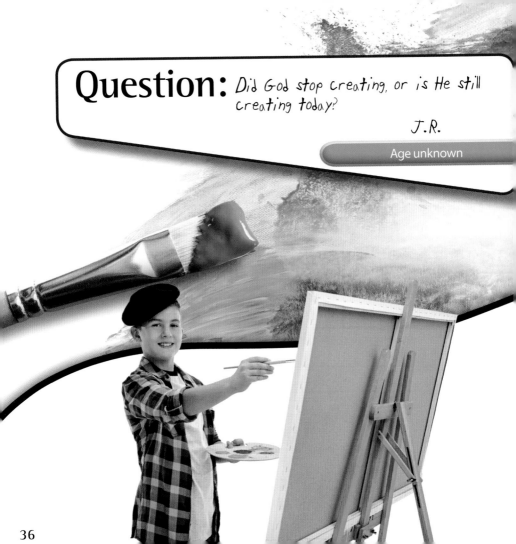

36

Answer:

For behold, I create new heavens and a new earth; and the former shall not be remembered or come to mind (Isaiah 65:17).

Creation week is over. God is no longer creating in the way that He did back then. In fact, God rested on the seventh day (called the Sabbath day) and instituted rest. This is why a seven-day week exists.

God didn't need to rest, but He did this as a pattern for us — the Sabbath day of rest was made for man, not man for the Sabbath (Mark 2:27). Just because God rested doesn't mean He is not active in His creation.

God still performed miraculous creations after creation week. For instance, Jesus created wine from water and food for 5,000 people. Also, Christians, as fallen and sinful people, are created new (Psalm 51:10). Second Corinthians 5:17 says:

Therefore, if anyone is in Christ, he is a new creation; old things have passed away; behold, all things have become new.

The Bible points out that when Jesus ascended into heaven, He went away to prepare a place for us. Yes, God is still active, and creating things is an easy task for an all-powerful God — who can do all His holy will.

John 14:2–3; Hebrews 1:3;
Revelation 4:11

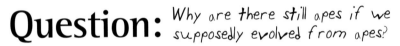

Question: Why are there still apes if we supposedly evolved from apes?

Grace

Age 11

Answer:

Test all things; hold fast what is good (1 Thessalonians 5:21).

There is a problem right from the start. There is the confusion over the word "ape." Allow me explain it like this: why are there still *modern apes like gorillas and chimpanzees* if we supposedly evolved from *ancient ape-like creatures that we call apes*?

The problem is that we called this alleged ape-like ancestor... an ape. The evolutionists believe this ape-like ancestor gave rise to modern apes — like the chimps and gorillas — but also gave rise to man. So evolutionists still expect modern apes to exist, even within their story.

The big problem is with *the evolutionary story*. When we test this story against the Bible, it fails. There are no ancient ape-like creatures long before apes and man. Both man and apes were made on the 6th day of creation.

What we find in the fossil record are apes and humans. Ape and human fossils are found in post-Flood rock (though it is possible that some could be found in Flood rock). The point is that Noah (and his family) and the two apes with him on the ark existed before these fossils were formed. Modern apes are descendants of the two that were on the ark.

Genesis 8:1; Ephesians 5:6;
Colossians 2:4

39

Question: Do all scientists believe in evolution?

Noah

Answer:

Teach me good judgment and knowledge, for I believe Your commandments (Psalm 119:66).

I (Bodie) am a scientist. I worked and taught in science for years developing new technology (materials and engineering). I do not believe in evolution. There are many scientists who believe evolution and there are many who do not. I know of thousands who do not believe in evolution.

Most fields of science ("knowledge") were actually developed by Bible-believing Christians. These include Isaac Newton (who was arguably the greatest scientist to ever live), Robert Boyle, Johannes Kepler, Galileo Galilei, Louis Pasteur, Gregor Mendel, and many more.

There are modern scientists who are Bible-believers too. For example there is Dr. Raymond Damadian, who invented a medical machine called an MRI. There is Dr. Jason Lisle (astrophysicist), Dr. Andrew Snelling (geologist), Dr. Danny Faulkner (astronomer), Dr. Tommy Mitchell (medical doctor), Dr. David Menton (anatomist), Dr. Georgia Purdom and Dr. Nathaniel Jeanson (geneticists), Dr. Stuart Burgess (engineer), Dr. David DeWitt (neuroscience), and many others.

Creationists recognize that God upholds all things in a consistent way. This is what makes observable and repeatable science possible. When we study God's creation using science, we like to say that we are "thinking God's thoughts after Him."

Proverbs 1:5, 17:24

Question:

Why do evolutionists believe in big bang?

Annie

Age 10

Answer:

By faith we understand that the worlds were framed by the word of God, so that the things which are seen were not made of things which are visible (Hebrews 11:3).

Evolution is built on the idea that there is no God who created in the past. All things had to come from somewhere, but evolutionists don't want God involved. So if God didn't create everything, then the only other option is to say things came about by themselves, without God.

This is what big bang is. It is a religious belief about origins that says there was nothing . . . then something popped into existence from nothing. This "cosmic egg" or "singularity" then rapidly expanded (exploded) and finally arrived at what we have today.

Keep in mind that no one has ever observed this and no one could recreate it. It is not science, but just a story (a myth) that some people came up with because they didn't want to trust what God says.

Sadly, some Christians try to add the big-bang myth to the Bible and say that God started the big bang. But this doesn't make sense, because God would NOT have created anything if the big bang happened. There is no reason to add this false story of the big bang to the Bible.

Nehemiah 9:6; Romans 12:2

Question: Do any evolutionists believe God is real, and is it okay to mix Christianity with evolution?

Neva & Reens

Ages 10

Answer:

Do not be deceived, God is not mocked; for whatever a man sows, that he will also reap (Galatians 6:7).

They are generally called "theistic evolutionists." Theistic means they believe in God. Basically, some Christians reject God's Word in Genesis and adopt the evolutionary story instead. This is inconsistent (not a good way to think).

What they are doing is mixing their Christianity with the religion of evolution, which is part of the religion of humanism/atheism.

In the Old Testament, godly Israelites started to worship "false gods" along with the true God. It was inconsistent for them to worship the true God, and then turn around and worship false gods. God was angry at the Israelites and judged them harshly!

Even the very wise and smart King Solomon began worshiping false gods. The Lord was angry with King Solomon too. Do you think God is angry when Christians mix their religion with false religions like humanism and evolution?

Christians should believe what God said about creation instead of believing evolution. God was there, and He knows what happened. There is no reason to trade what God said in Genesis for the false religion of evolution.

1 King 9:6–9

45

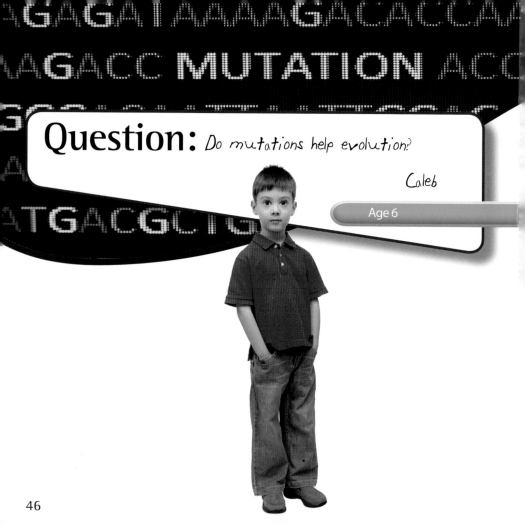

Question: Do mutations help evolution?

Caleb

Age 6

Answer:

His parents answered them and said, "We know that this is our son, and that he was born blind" (John 9:20).

Mutations are mistakes in your DNA (the code that builds your body). They can cause serious diseases or cause people to have problems with their arms, legs, or other parts of their body — like being born blind!

Evolution teaches that a single-celled organism — like an amoeba — changed (by mutation) into all the animals that we have today. For the "amoeba" to change into a dog (over long ages), it would have to mutate the DNA to get information for hair, eyes, lungs, nerves, blood, and so on. But mutations don't produce things like this.

Instead, mutations actually cause big problems. Mutations create problems that cause the animal to be broken. They are hailed as the hero for evolution, but mutations actually destroy animals and cause big problems.

Mutations are real, but they are problems that are not helpful. Mutations are part of a broken world that happened as a result of sin in Genesis 3. In heaven, we won't have to worry about this anymore.

2 Samuel 21:20; Revelation 21:4

Answers Are Always Important!

The Bible is truly filled some amazing answers for some of our toughest faith questions. The Answers Book for Kids series answers questions from children around the world in this multi-volume series. Each volume will answer over 20 questions in a friendly and readable style appropriate for children 6–12 years old; and each covers a unique topic, including Creation and the Fall; Dinosaurs and the Flood of Noah; God and the Bible; and Sin, Salvation, and the Christian Life, and more!

[1] L. Xing, P. Bell, W. Persons, S. Ji, T. Miyashita, et al., abdominal contents from two large early Cretaceous compsognathids (Dinosauria: Theropoda) demonstate feeding on confuciusornithids and dromaeosaurids, PLoS ONE 7(8): e44012. doi:10.1371/journal.pone.0044012, August 29, 2012.